Terrible Times

Blitz Britain

Une histoire terriblement racontée par
Philippa Boston
et illustrée par Mark Beech

didier

paper planes *teens*

Une collection imaginée avec humour, enthousiasme et provocation par Rupert Morgan

Tous les titres que vous pourrez ~~enfin~~ lire en anglais !

Débutant
A1→A2

- What is Brian? *Rupert Morgan*
- Welcome to Star School, *Michaela Morgan*
- Panic at Star School, *Michaela Morgan*
- Star School on Tour, *Michaela Morgan*

Intermédiaire
A2→B1

- Macbeth and the Creature from Hell, *Roger Morris*
- Romeo and Juliet in Las Vegas, *Rupert Morgan*
- Bubonic Britain, *Philippa Boston*
- Deadly Jobs, *Philippa Boston*
- Blitz Britain, *Philippa Boston*
- Killer Sports, *Philippa Boston*

Avancé
B1→B2

- Frankenstein 2.0, *Roger Morris*
- Facebook Dracula, *Peter Flynn*
- Live Fast, Die Young, *Rupert Morgan*
- Rock Rebels, *Rupert Morgan*

Direction artistique : Mandy Norman
Maquette intérieure et composition : Becky Chilcott
Édition : Catherine Laurent, Sandrine Paniel
Enregistrements : Studio Corby
p. 17 : Keystone/Gettyimages ; p. 18 : Pictorial Press/Alamy

 – ISBN 978-2-278-07937-7 – ISSN 2271-7269
Dépôt légal : 7937/01 – Achevé d'imprimer en Italie en mars 2014 par Grafica Veneta

TERRIBLE TIMES

BLITZ BRITAIN

PART ONE
The Terrifying Truth

Do you think only soldiers die in wars? Think again. In World War 2, German bombers attacked British cities night after night, destroying nearly **two million homes**! You never knew, going to bed, if you would be alive in the morning...

➤ **pages 5–29**

PART TWO
A Sensational Story!

Teenager Billy just wants to go home after work on a dark winter evening. But he has to cross London during the **biggest attack** of the Blitz. Soon Billy is part of a night of **extraordinary heroism**. A story inspired by true events.

➤ **pages 31–48**

PART ONE

THE TERRIFYING TRUTH

What was the Blitz?

The Blitz was total, no-rules war.

It was a new military tactic invented by Germany under Adolf Hitler in 1940: the massive bombardment of British cities at night by the Luftwaffe, the German air force.

The plan was to destroy Britain's infrastructure and break the nation's morale before an invasion from France.

But the invasion never happened. Why? Well, that's the story of the Blitz...

The Children's Evacuation

As soon as war was declared, the British government evacuated all the children from dangerous areas. Almost immediately, three and a half million children from the cities were transported to villages, where it was safe.

Each child had just *one* bag and a label around their neck with their name and address.

The children didn't know where they were going. Often, in the chaos of the evacuation, not even the adults in charge knew! Convoys just took the first train out of London!

When the children arrived in a village, the local families chose which child they wanted. Most children stayed with nice families, but some families were horrible and made them work like slaves.

So why were there still so many children in the cities during the Blitz? Firstly, because some parents refused to let their children be evacuated. Secondly, it was some months before the bombing started and many evacuated children were so unhappy that they returned home...

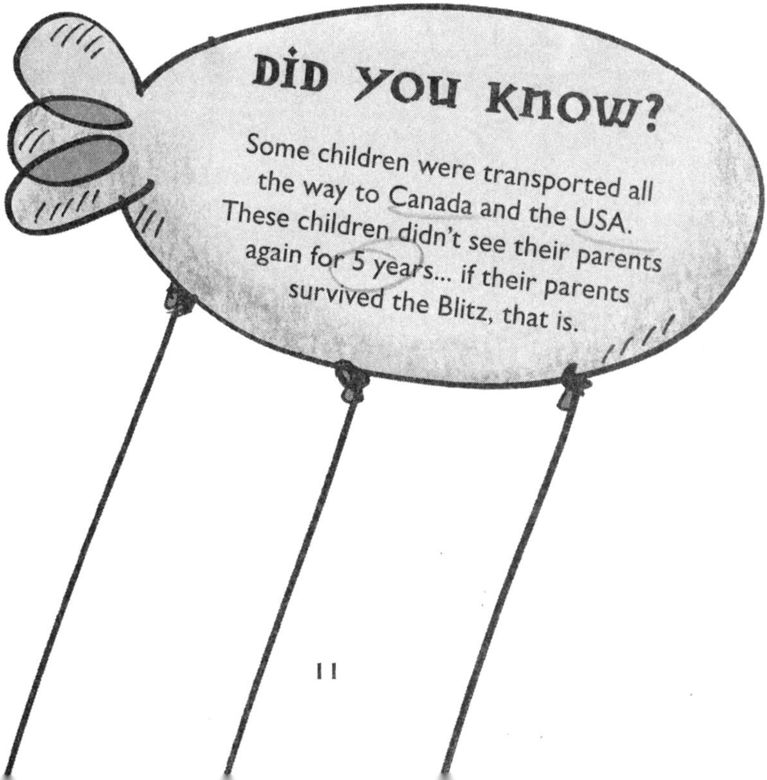

The Blitz begins...

JULY 19, 1940

The Daily News

BRITAIN SAYS NO TO HITLER'S PEACE OFFER!

The government says there can be no peace when Germany still occupies France and the rest of Europe!

At 5pm on 7th September 1940, the first planes arrived over central London and began to drop bombs. In the next few hours, 600 more bomber planes arrived...

That night, the city was on fire along 14km of the river Thames!

The Germans continued bombing every night for 76 nights. They didn't just bomb London, but all towns where there were ports or armaments factories.

So... the British bombed German cities too. The death and destruction on both sides was devastating. This is why, when you visit German or British cities today, most of the buildings are not very old...

KNOW YOUR BOMBS!

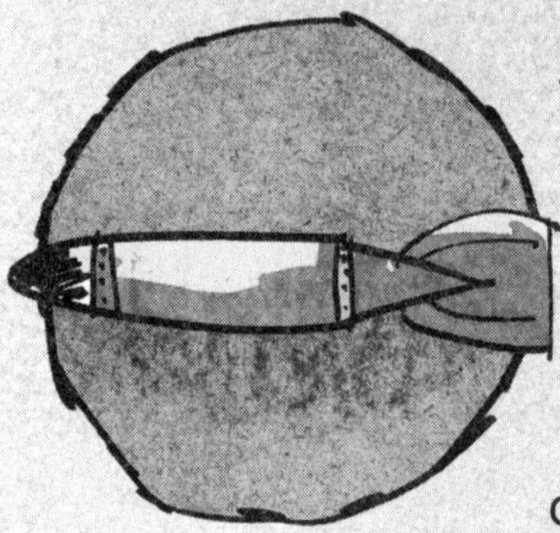

INCENDIARY BOMBS

These were dropped first. They were small aluminium tubes that did not explode, but made fire. This was so that the German bomber pilots could see their targets at night.

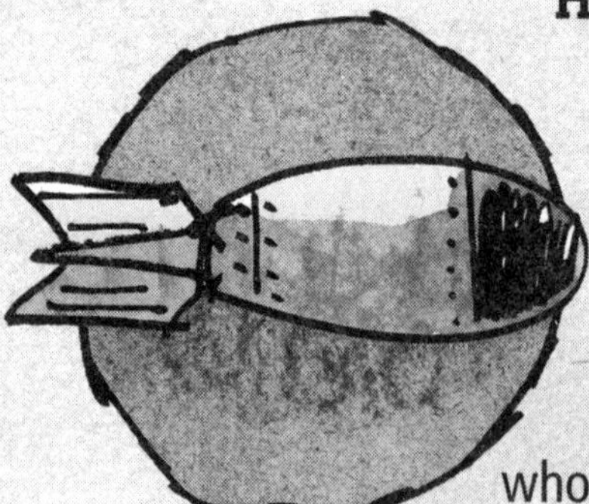

HIGH EXPLOSIVE BOMBS

These were of different sizes, from 50 kg to 500 kg. The biggest of them all was called The Blockbuster, which was powerful enough to destroy a whole block of houses or a factory.

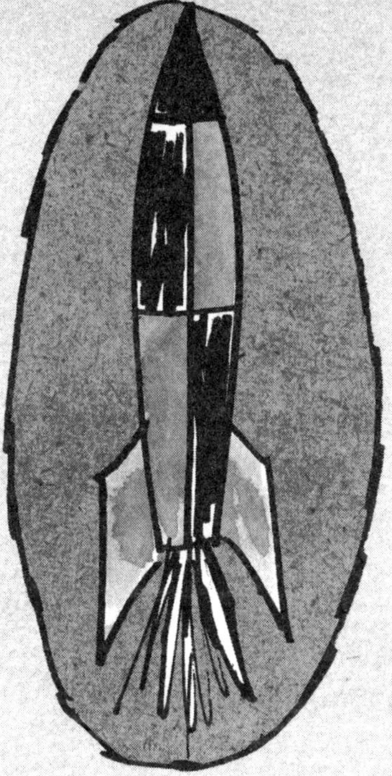

V-2 ROCKETS

The world's first ballistic missiles, these were only invented later in the war. They began to land on London in 1944. By then, Germany was losing the war. The V stands for *Vergeltungswaffe*, or "Vengeance Weapon".

DID YOU KNOW?

The V-2 is the mother of all space rockets. After the war, the German missile scientists were taken to the USA and the Soviet Union to work on their space programmes. The Apollo rocket that took man to the moon was designed by Wernher von Braun, the creator of the V-2 missile, and used the same technology.

Are German planes dropping bombs in your street?

Protect your family with

THE BLITZ SURVIVAL KIT!!!

☞ **AN ANDERSON SHELTER!**

Build it in the garden of your home!

☞ **GAS MASKS!**
Never go anywhere without them!

☞ **Now you can get a gas mask for your dog!**
(Note: A feline version is not availabe, but cats have nine lives anyway.)

☞ **DIG FOR VICTORY!**
Everyone must grow vegetables in their garden!

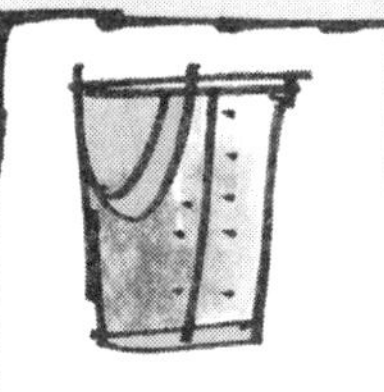

☞ **A BUCKET OF WATER to put out fire!**

☞ **There's nothing like a good CUP OF TEA to steady your nerves!**

☞ **CANDLES AND TORCHES! But make sure those German pilots don't see your light!**

How to Sleep in an Air Raid

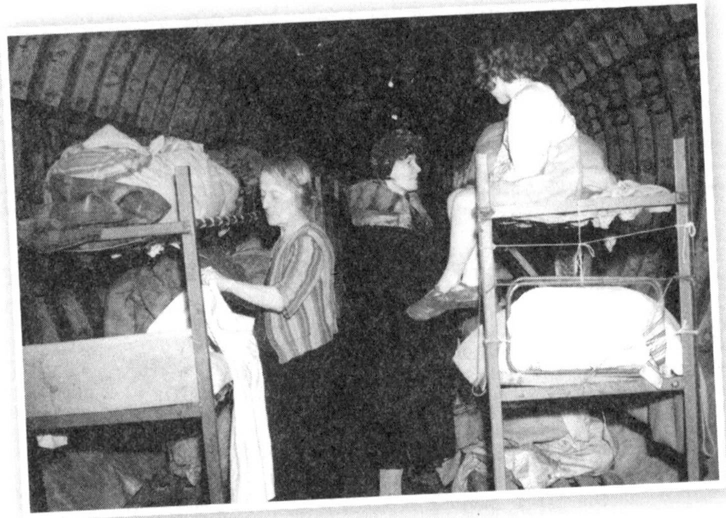

London did not have many public air raid shelters, so people started to use the Underground System for protection!

At first the government tried to stop this, but in the end they gave up and let people sleep on the platforms of the Underground every night. There were beds, people would sing and play music, and volunteers distributed tea and food.

Instead of an Anderson Shelter in their garden, many people had something called a Morrison Shelter *inside* their house. This looked like a big metal table. They slept inside and it was supposed to protect them if a bomb hit their house.

How to Hide a City

After dark, there was a total blackout all over Britain. This was so that the German bombers could not see their targets.

Everyone put black curtains on the windows of their houses to block the light.

Smokers were told to hide their cigarettes with their hands if planes were in the sky.

And cars drove with no headlights. Unsurprisingly, there were a lot of accidents.

London Zoo in the Blitz

London Zoo is in Regent's Park, in the heart of London. This caused a few problems...

A bomb fell on the monkey house, but no monkeys were injured. They were intelligent enough to take shelter during air raids! Apparently, they had a lot of fun playing on the rubble the next morning.

In one bomb attack, some of the animals escaped. For a while, zebras were living free in Regent's Park!
Fortunately, in case this happened, the big predators had been evacuated to rural areas just like the children.
Dangerous snakes and spiders were not so lucky as the big cats. They were euthanised at the start of the war.
Still, most of London's zoo animals were luckier than those in Paris: they were *eaten* during the war!

Buckingham Palace in the Blitz

At the start of the Blitz, the government suggested that the princesses, Elizabeth and Margaret, should be evacuated to Canada.

"The children won't go without me", the Queen said. "I won't leave without the King. And the King will *never* leave."

So, although they had homes all over Britain, the Royal Family chose Buckingham Palace as their official residence during the war, to show solidarity with ordinary citizens.

This demonstration of solidarity is a big reason why the Royal Family are so popular in Britain today.

When Buckingham Palace was damaged by a bomb, the Queen said she was pleased because now she could look Londoners from the East End* in the eye!

* The east of London, called the East End, is traditionally working class. Buckingham Palace is in the richer West End. The east is where the docks were, and was very heavily bombed.

When she was old enough, Princess Elizabeth (today's Queen Elizabeth II) joined the army and worked as a mechanic during the war.

What Can YOU Do in the War?

Can't join the army and fight?
Don't worry, there's plenty for you to do!

Become a **Land Girl**! Over 80,000 women have joined the Women's Land Army to work on farms while the men are at war!

Too old to fight? Then join the **Home Guard**! If the Germans invade, then you will be our last line of defence!

Become an **Air Raid Warden**! Make sure people obey the black-out and know where to go during an air raid!

Even children are doing their part! Children all over the country are **collecting scrap metal** for armaments, and schools are **growing vegetables** to feed the nation!

How Did It End?

After nine months of nightly attacks that left 375,000 Londoners homeless, Hitler stopped the Blitz because the tactic was not a success. Germany had lost over 2,200 planes, but Britain's infrastructure was still operational.

And, instead of breaking the country's morale, the Blitz had the opposite effect: it reinforced everyone's determination to resist Germany at all costs, even though Britain had no allies at this point in the war.

Today, it is celebrated as a time when ordinary people acted with extraordinary fortitude* and heroism.

Fortunately, the USA and the Soviet Union entered the war in 1941. After that, things started to go badly for Hitler...

* **fortitude:** *force morale*

The Germans are having a world war... and nobody invited US?

PART TWO

THE LONGEST NIGHT

A STORY INSPIRED BY TRUE EVENTS

Chapter 1

Life in Wartime

London, December 29th, 1940

All the young men are fighting in the war, so it was easy for me to get a job even though I'm only 14. I work with my dad at Smithfield meat market.

Meat is rationed because of the war. First it was petrol. Then bacon, sugar.... now just about *everything* is rationed!

Except fish. We can eat all the fish our boats can catch if the Jerry* submarines don't sink them. The fish is sold in Billingsgate Market, down by the river. They're doing good business there.

Because of the rationing, there are government inspectors everywhere at Smithfield Market.

*The British often nicknamed the Germans 'Jerries'.

Even so, Dad and I make sure our family and friends don't go hungry. We're very popular in our street at the moment!

Today, we had five pigs arriving from a farm in Norfolk. They were supposed to arrive at dawn, but the roads are icy and the driver didn't get here until midday.

It's 3 o'clock when I start my deliveries. I bicycle into the West End and it is almost dark when I arrive at the service entrance of the most luxurious hotel in London: the Savoy!

I don't like to be out after dark. That's when the Jerry bombers come...

Chapter 2
The Savoy Hotel

Because of the blackout, there are no streetlights after dark, so it's almost impossible to find your way around. And if you are in a strange part of town, you have no idea where the bomb shelters are.

At the Savoy, they're pleased to see me with all that pork! One of the chefs comes to the kitchen door to take a look at the meat.

"That, my lad, is fine fresh pork," he smiles. He takes it from me and gives it to one of the kitchen boys.

"Wait here!" the chef says.

I'm nervous because it's getting dark quickly, but soon he comes back and gives me a brown paper package.

"What's this?" I ask politely.

"That, lad, is for you and your father," he whispers. "It's a Christmas cake we made for one of the Greek princes staying upstairs. He said he didn't want it. You take it and enjoy it."

I gasp with surprise and happiness. But just then, it starts: the air raid siren.

"Come inside, lad," the chef says. "You'll be safer down here than on the street."

Chapter 3

Night Bombers

The chef tells me to sit in a corner and not get in anyone's way. The kitchens are underground, so they are a natural shelter and the cooks just keep on cooking as the bombs fall.

At home, when the Jerry bombers come, we go to our Anderson Shelter in the garden. At this time of year, it's freezing. And you can't sleep because the noise of the bombs is too loud. We live in the East End, close to the docks, so our part of town is always hit bad.

But here I am, sheltering in the Savoy Hotel, your majesty! Can you believe it?

I start talking to a kitchen boy who was about to go home when the sirens started. He's called

Danny. We talk about his job, and mine, and what we're going to do to the Jerries when we're old enough to join the army.

Danny lives near me, so we decide to go home together on my bicycle and show the Jerries we're not afraid. We come out of the hotel, and that's when we see it...

Chapter 4

London Burning

As soon as we step out of the Savoy, we realise that tonight is different.

I've seen some bad bombing, but not like this. Jerry's done a good job tonight. The whole bloody city is on fire. The Savoy is on the Thames, and the river is bright with the reflections of the flames.

I put my precious cake in my bag and tell Danny to sit on the front of my bicycle. We set off, laughing like a couple of crazy people because the bike is so unstable.

As we travel East, there is a massive wall of fire in front of us. So I turn left, thinking I can go around it, but as we turn into Shoe Lane we hear the sound of a whistle.

"You lads!" cries an Air Raid Warden. "Get back! Now! Move your arses!"

We turn back toward the Thames. Behind us, there is a noise like I've never heard before and a massive conflagration. I look over my shoulder and see that the book depots are on fire. There are tens of thousands of books in those buildings.

I don't mind admitting that we're pretty scared at this point. On one side of us there is the fire, on the other side is the river. It's vital that we do not become trapped, forced to choose between burning to death or drowning in the river.

Chapter 5

The Fight for Saint Paul's

I go down Fleet Street, toward St Paul's cathedral. I've never pedalled so fast. Danny holds on for dear life as bombs fall all around us. My ears hurt from the noise of the explosions.

Passing St Paul's, we see people up on the roof. They are running this way and that with buckets of water, trying to save the building.

Danny and I look at each other. We both know what the other's thinking. We can't just go home. We have to help.

I leave my bike against the wall of the Cathedral, and we go inside. People with buckets and fire blankets are running in all directions.

"What can we do?" I shout at the nearest man.

He hands me and Danny two buckets.

"Fill these with water from the font – over there – and take them up to the roof."

We go to work. Up and down, up and down those stairs, carrying buckets of water to the men on the roof. For hours, we don't stop to rest.

Despite our efforts, the situation just gets worse. A wind starts, and that creates a firestorm in the city. By midnight, every single building around St Paul's is on fire. Up on the roof, we are surrounded by a solid wall of flame.

Then – disaster! An incendiary bomb lands on the dome. It starts to burn through the lead like butter. On the other side, the dome is built from wood. If the flames get inside, the whole cathedral will go up like a box of matches...

Chapter 6

The Man with no Name

No one knows who he is, but he's a hero. A real one.

Knowing the incendiary bomb is about to melt through the dome, Danny and I ran inside. And that's when we saw him: the silhouette of a man moving along the rafters[1] like a circus tightrope walker[2].

One foot wrong, and he'll fall to his death. I don't think anyone breathes as we watch him. He moves forward, step by step, until he gets to where the bomb is burning through the lead.

He has a stick in his hand. He pokes the bomb with it, like someone trying to push a football out of a tree. Poke... poke... and then the bomb moves. He's done it! He's pushed the bomb off the dome!

1. **rafters:** *poutres*
2. **tightrope walker:** *funambule*

It rolls down the dome, and then the men on the roof throw water on it to extinguish the fire.

After that, we work even harder. At one point the flames are so close that I think we must all be going to die. But, somehow, the cathedral never catches fire. I don't know why. God maybe? God, and a whole army of us with our buckets and fire blankets.

Chapter Seven

The Next Day

I don't know how we find our way home. The bombing has caused such devastation that nothing looks the same. You can't say which street is which anymore. It's all gone. Destroyed.

Finally, we get home to Stepney. Danny and I shake hands and laugh at each other, realising we are as black as a couple of chimney sweeps. We agree to meet again next Sunday.

When I walk into the kitchen, everyone is just sitting there: Mum, Dad, Shirley, Tom, Burt and Mabel. Sitting there in silence, all thinking I must be dead. I can see they have been crying.

Mum looks at me as if she has seen a ghost, cries out my name and throws her arms around me.

And then the rest of them all join in, all crying as they hold me!

"Don't be silly!" I say. "You'll all get dirty, and then Mum will have more washing to do."

As soon as they let go of me, I ask if there's any chance of a cup of tea. And Mum really laughs then, and puts the kettle on.

That's when I open my bag.

"Because I've got something to go with it," I say, and I lift out the parcel that has survived the second Great Fire of London*. "Go on mum, open it."

*The first Great Fire of London was in 1666 and destroyed much of the city.

She undoes the parcel, very slowly. And when the cake appears, they all start shouting and jumping around in excitement. And I watch them, laughing.

And do you know what? I don't think I'll *ever* eat anything that tastes as good as that cake does, on the morning of 30th December, 1940.